Looking at Maps

Written and Illustrated by Erich Fuchs

Editorial direction · Barbara Fenton

First United States Publication, 1976

Library of Congress Catalog Card Number: 75-42554
ISBN: 0-200-00167-1 RB

Printed in Great Britain

Abelard-Schuman

New York

This is Ben Willis.

Ben lives in a room that looks like this,

in a house that looks like this,

on a street that looks like this,

in a town that looks like this, called Redford,
which is in a county called Millstone,
which is in a country called Peacedom.

So Ben's address is: Ben's Room
                     38 Garden Street
                     Redford, Millstone
                     Peacedom

3

Can we say any more about *where* Ben lives? His room is the smallest thing in Ben's address, his country the biggest, but even his country is part of still bigger things. Peacedom is only one country on the continent of Middleland, which is part of the whole Earth. The Earth is only one planet among many that revolve around the sun to make our Solar System. The Solar System is part of a Galaxy of many suns (stars), and beyond that is the whole Universe of countless galaxies and vast space.

So we can write Ben's *whole* address, going from little to big, like this:

Your own address would have a different house, street, town, county, country and continent, but you too live on Earth, in the Solar System, in the Milky Way Galaxy, in the Universe. What is *your* whole address?

If we imagine a visitor from another galaxy in the Universe, looking for Ben, he would need Ben's address and then some maps. An address *tells* where things are, a map *shows* where they are.

A map of the Universe shows millions of galaxies, some only distant pinpoints of light. Among them is our visitor's own, and Ben's and our own Milky Way Galaxy.

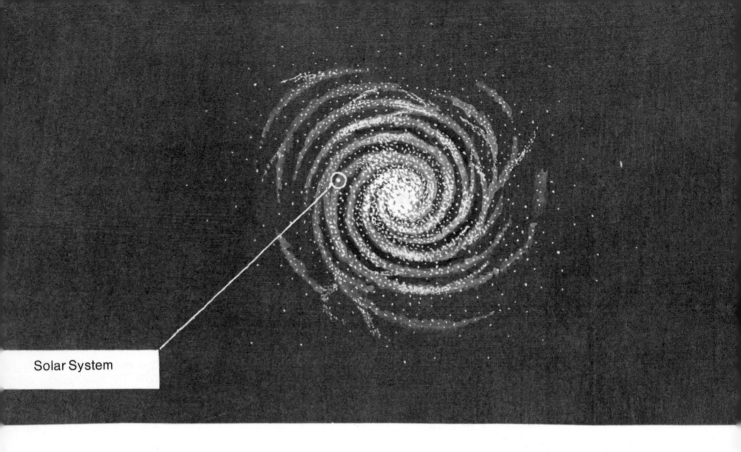

Solar System

Once in the right Galaxy, a larger map of it alone is needed to find the Solar System.

An even larger map of the Solar System alone shows the planets, including Earth.

distances and siz
not to scale

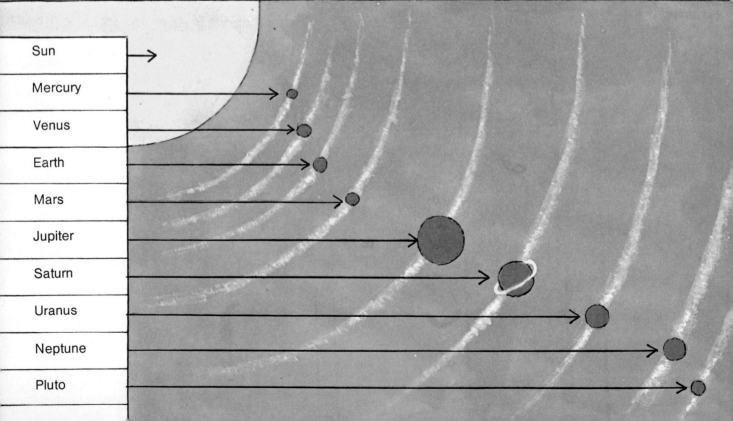

| Sun |
| Mercury |
| Venus |
| Earth |
| Mars |
| Jupiter |
| Saturn |
| Uranus |
| Neptune |
| Pluto |

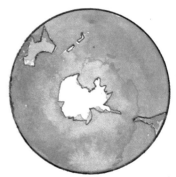

Now our visitor wants a map of just the Earth. But the Earth is a round ball. How can we see all of its sides? A *globe* is a round ball, like the Earth, and on it we can show the Earth's lands as they really are. Here are different views of the same globe.

But if we want to show the whole Earth on flat paper we have to draw a *projection,* which is simply a globe cut into sections and laid flat. One way to do it is shown below.

All maps really are parts of a projected globe, and because they are flat drawings of a rounded piece of Earth they are always somewhat distorted. You cannot flatten a curved surface without some pushing and pulling and filling in of gaps. Try peeling an orange in one continuous piece and placing the peel flat on a table–you will see the problem.

Peacedom

Back to our search for Ben. Now that we are on Earth we need a still larger map of Ben's continent with his country on it.

Next, a large map of Ben's country shows his county and his town, but it is not large enough to show his town as anything more than a dot, so

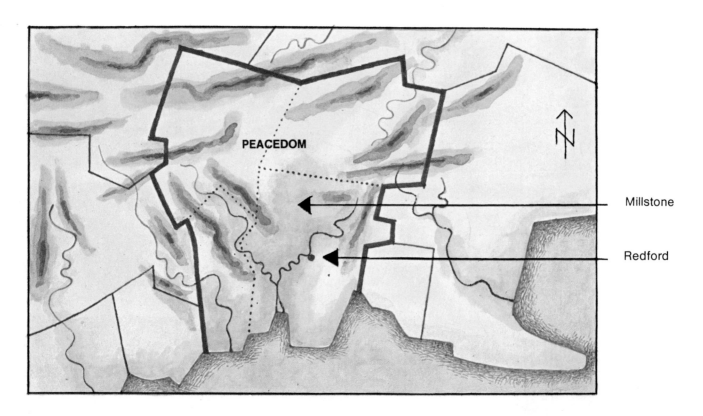

PEACEDOM

Millstone

Redford

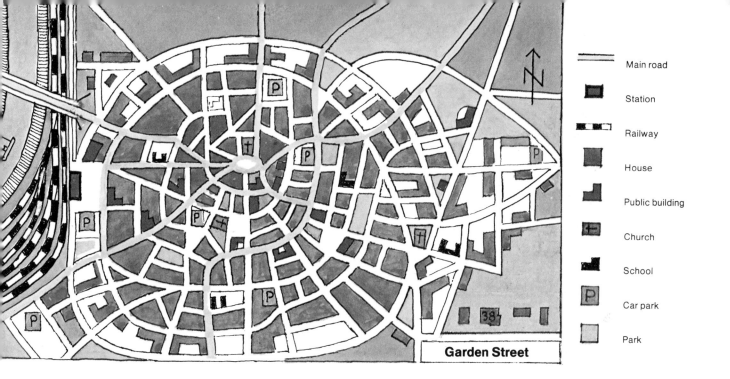

Main road

Station

Railway

House

Public building

Church

School

Car park

Park

Garden Street

we take a larger map of the town and on it we can find Ben's street, Garden Street, and even Ben's house.

Below is a map of the first floor of Ben's house. It is called a plan. And finally a map, or plan, of Ben's room. Compare it with the picture on page 2. And now we have found Ben–sitting at his desk. X marks the spot on the plan!

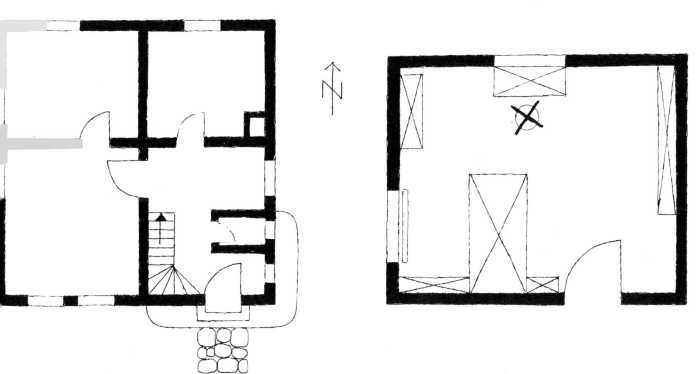

It took many maps to find Ben because we started with the whole gigantic Universe. In comparison to the size of the Universe Ben was only a tiny speck and wouldn't have been visible on such *small-scale* maps.

Small-scale means that the map is very much smaller than the actual thing or area it describes–scale means comparison between map size and real size. A small-scale map cannot show many details.

On a *large-scale* map there is less difference between the actual thing and the map of it, so the map can show more and smaller details.

The map of Ben's room was large-scale–only about 60 times smaller than his room. The map of his country was small-scale–perhaps 5,000,000 (5 million) times smaller than the real thing. We say the scale of the room plan was 1:60, the scale of the country map 1:5,000,000.

Another way to say this is that one millimeter (0.004 inch) on the plan equals 60 millimeters (0.24 inch) of the real room – or one plan centimeter (0.39 inch) equals 6 room centimeters (2.34 room inches). You can measure a distance on any map, then compare it to the bar scale to find the real land distance.

Ben's country is only a pretend country–there is no real country called Peacedom, no continent called Middleland. But in the last pages of this book you will see maps of the real countries of your part of the world, and they will be 15 million times smaller than the real thing–they will be in a scale of 1:15,000,000.

Here are three maps of the same area, each in a different scale. As the scale gets larger we see more details than we could see on the previous map.

Town

 Motorway/Tunnel

Street

Railway

 Canal

 Lake

 River

Marsh

 Wood

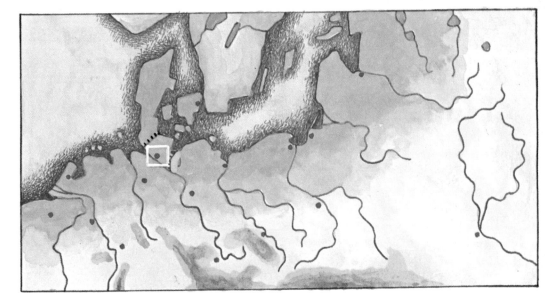

```
      100   200
                  km
      62    124 miles
  Scale 1: 15,000,000
```

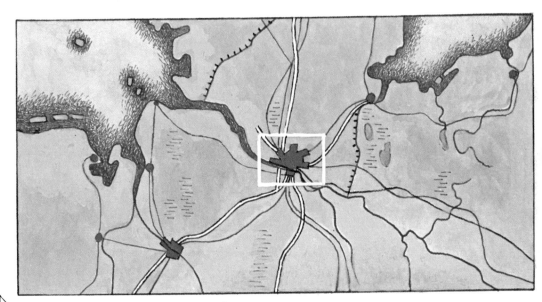

```
        50          100
                         km
        31 miles       62 miles
  Scale 1: 2,250,000
```

```
      5    10    15
                    km
      3.1 miles  6.2 miles  9.3 miles
  Scale 1: 500,000
```

11

So far we have seen that maps are useful for showing where places are (and even where a person is!). But maps have many other uses. The same map outline, of a country, for instance, can be filled with almost anything we want to tell about the country. For this we use *symbols*. Symbols may resemble the real thing, like these for mountain, river, and roads.

Or they may just be convenient little signs that don't look much like what they stand for:

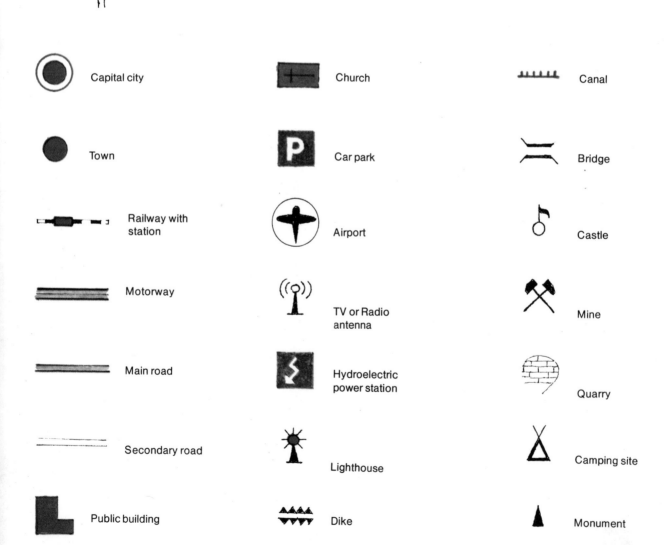

◉	Capital city	▬	Church	⬩⬩⬩⬩⬩⬩	Canal
●	Town	P	Car park	⌣	Bridge
▸■◂	Railway with station	✈	Airport	♪	Castle
═	Motorway	((☉))	TV or Radio antenna	⚒	Mine
─	Main road	⚡	Hydroelectric power station	▱	Quarry
─	Secondary road	☀	Lighthouse	△	Camping site
◪	Public building	▲▼	Dike	▲	Monument

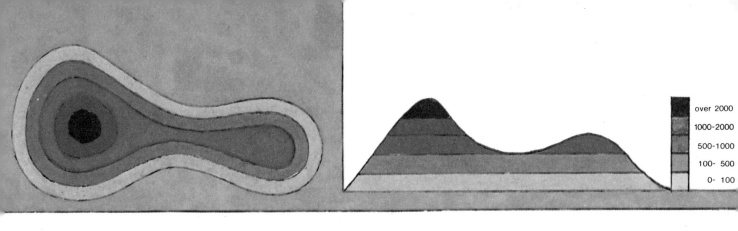

over 2000	
1000-2000	
500-1000	
100- 500	
0- 100	

Another way of symbolizing mountains is with contours, which are lines connecting all points of the same height (above sea level).

Color is also used to give information on maps. Water is usually blue, and land is shown in a range of colors according to its height, with patterns for the different kinds of natural vegetation (plant life).

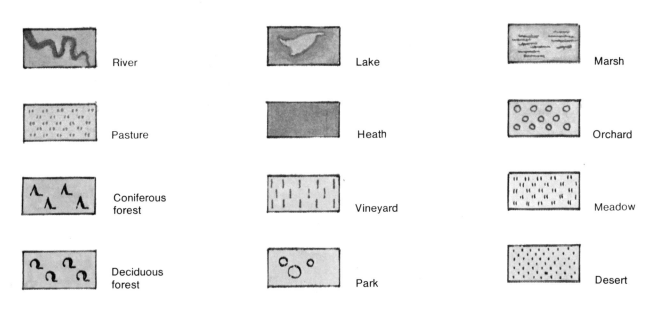

River   Lake   Marsh

Pasture   Heath   Orchard

Coniferous forest   Vineyard   Meadow

Deciduous forest   Park   Desert

On a map of many countries, where it is important to see where each country starts and ends, a different color is used for each. This is called a *political map*.

100 200
km
62 124 miles
Scale 1: 20,000,000

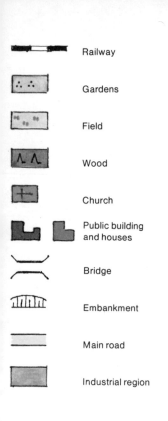

Railway

Gardens

Field

Wood

Church

Public building and houses

Bridge

Embankment

Main road

Industrial region

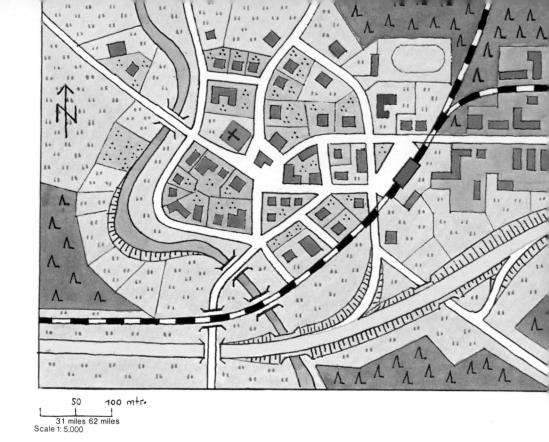

50   100 mtr.
31 miles 62 miles
Scale 1: 5,000

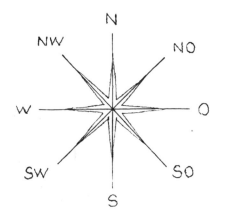

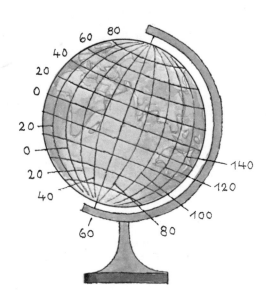

On most maps, a box called a key or legend lists and explains all the symbols and colors used, and notes the scale. The scale may be written as a comparison (1:5,000 on this map) or shown on a bar scale that allows you to figure actual distance by measuring distance on the map. If you cut a piece of paper the length of your bar scale, you can move it about on your map as needed.

This compass rose, found on many maps, tells which way on the map is north (usually at the top), which south, east and west.

Maps and globes have lines drawn on them to help us locate places. Longitude lines (meridians) circle the globe running north and south and meeting at the poles. Latitude lines (parallels) run east and west above and below the equator, the imaginary line around the middle of the Earth. Numbers on the meridians and parallels tell us exactly where to find any place on Earth.

Symbols and color, then, make it possible for us to use the same map outline to show almost anything we want.

A *road map* shows the roads in an area and is helpful to travelers. A small-scale road map will show only main roads, but a large-scale road map will show all the little roads as well.

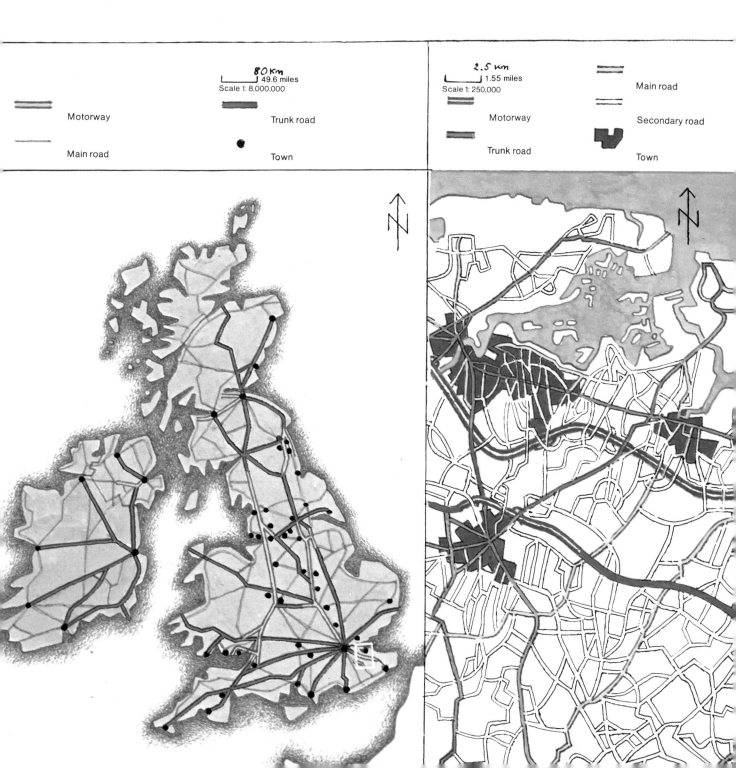

Motorway

Main road

80 Km
49.6 miles
Scale 1: 8,000,000

Trunk road

Town

2.5 Km
1.55 miles
Scale 1: 250,000

Motorway

Trunk road

Main road

Secondary road

Town

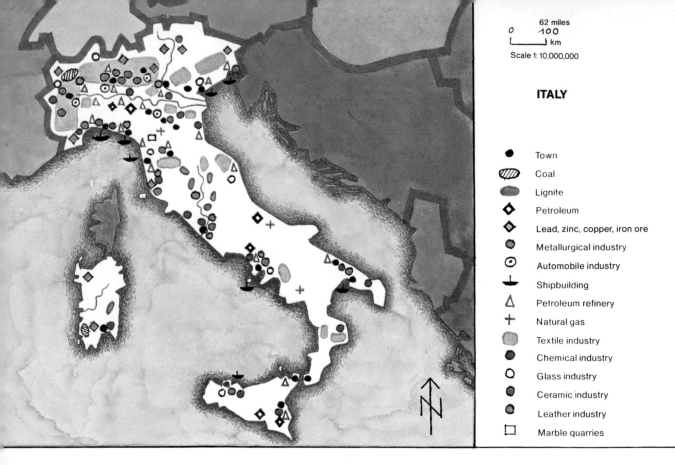

62 miles
0   100
        km
Scale 1: 10,000,000

ITALY

● Town
▨ Coal
▬ Lignite
◇ Petroleum
◆ Lead, zinc, copper, iron ore
◉ Metallurgical industry
◉ Automobile industry
⊥ Shipbuilding
△ Petroleum refinery
+ Natural gas
▬ Textile industry
● Chemical industry
○ Glass industry
● Ceramic industry
● Leather industry
▭ Marble quarries

A *product map* shows all the things an area manufactures or grows, and in what places.

A *physical map* reveals the nature of the land–its mountains, rivers, plains, valleys and other features.

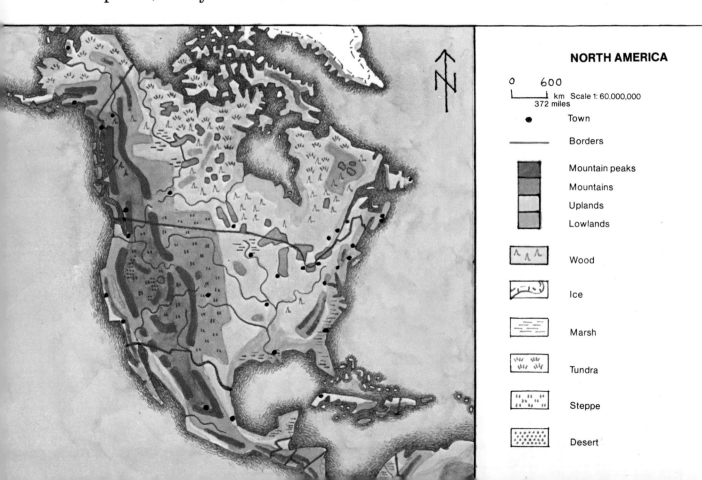

NORTH AMERICA

0   600
        km Scale 1: 60,000,000
372 miles

● Town
— Borders

Mountain peaks
Mountains
Uplands
Lowlands

Wood

Ice

Marsh

Tundra

Steppe

Desert

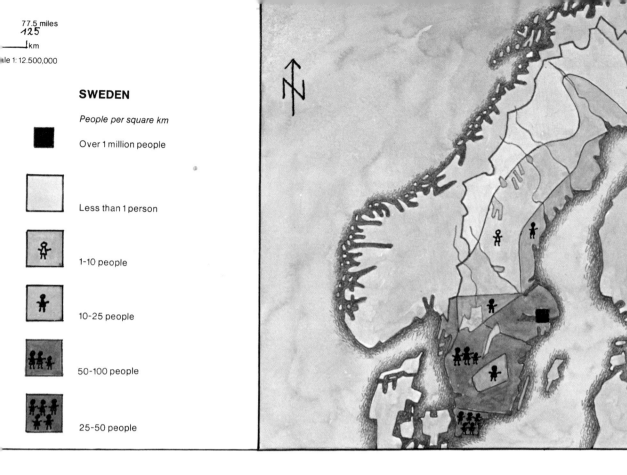

SWEDEN

People per square km

■ Over 1 million people

☐ Less than 1 person

1-10 people

10-25 people

50-100 people

25-50 people

Symbols on a map can be used to show the number of people living
in different parts of a country, as well as the areas in which different
languages are spoken.

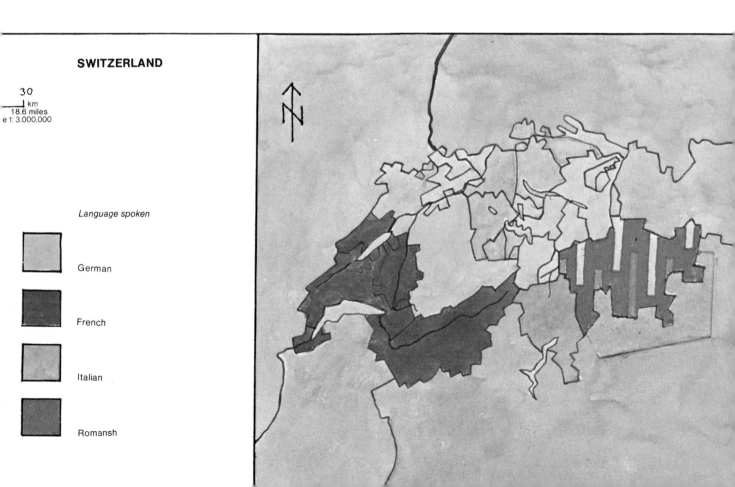

SWITZERLAND

30
km
18.6 miles
e 1: 3.000,000

Language spoken

☐ German

French

Italian

Romansh

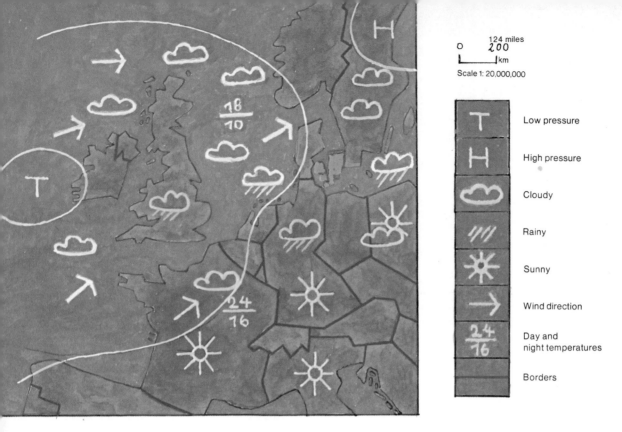

T	Low pressure
H	High pressure
☁	Cloudy
///	Rainy
☀	Sunny
→	Wind direction
24/16	Day and night temperatures
	Borders

The changing weather is recorded on a *climate* or *weather* map.

We have maps of the moon because even before man landed there he was able to study its details through a telescope. We weren't able to see enough of the surfaces of planets other than Earth, however, to have very detailed maps of them, but modern space probes are already changing that.

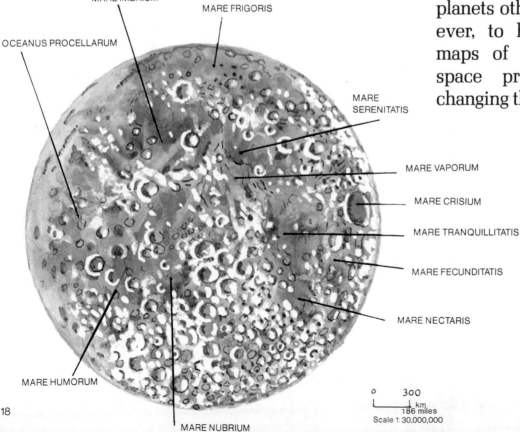

MARE IMBRIUM
MARE FRIGORIS
OCEANUS PROCELLARUM
MARE SERENITATIS
MARE VAPORUM
MARE CRISIUM
MARE TRANQUILLITATIS
MARE FECUNDITATIS
MARE NECTARIS
MARE HUMORUM
MARE NUBRIUM

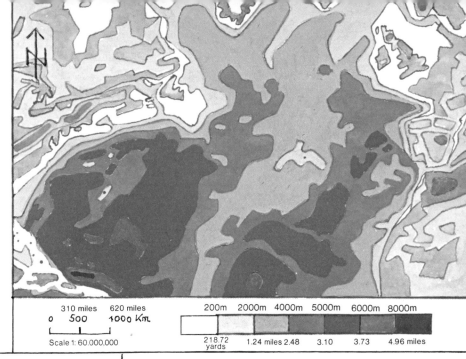

Our maps of the world's oceans, with their varying patterns of depths, tell us of equally strange landscapes under the waters.

310 miles	620 miles
0 500 1000 Km.	

Scale 1: 60.000.000

200m	2000m	4000m	5000m	6000m	8000m
218.72 yards	1.24 miles	2.48	3.10	3.73	4.96 miles

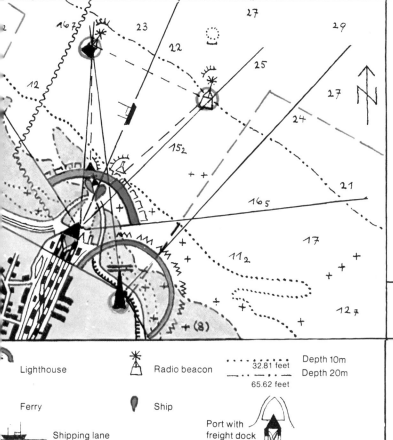

But to sail safely on the surface, a *navigation map* or *chart* is needed.

Lighthouse

Radio beacon

Depth 10m
Depth 20m

32.81 feet

65.62 feet

Ferry

Ship

Shipping lane

Port with freight dock

Airport with air traffic control center

Airway

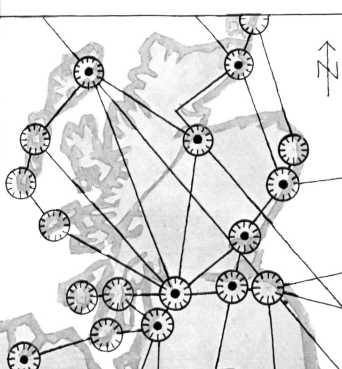

Pilots have similar charts of the skies showing safe paths for flight.

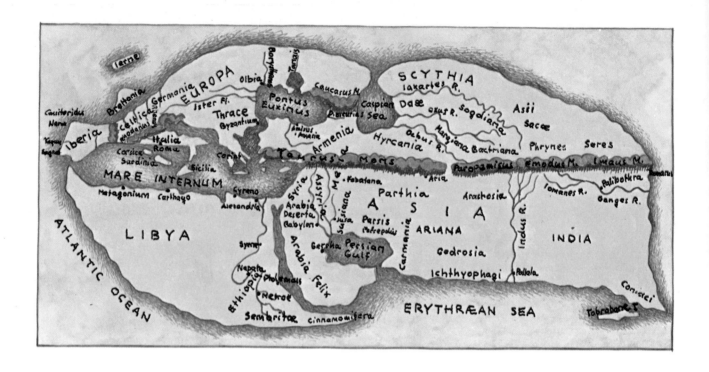

A *historical,* or *antique map* shows the world as it was centuries ago, or as people thought it looked before it was fully explored.

A map of a building, called a *plan* or *blueprint,* is a guide for workers during construction.

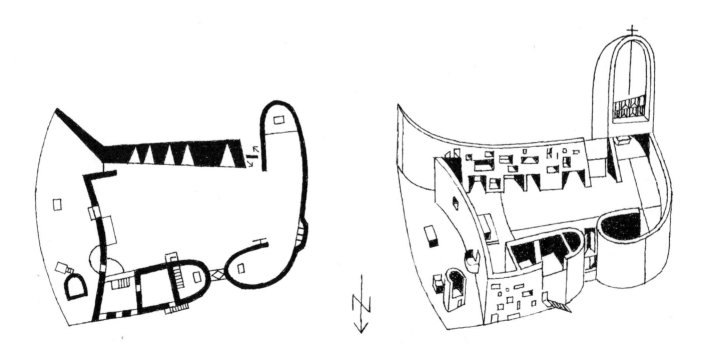

There is almost no end to the things maps can tell us. With a map you can find your way around a strange city, learn where to dig for buried treasure (if you were lucky enough to find an old pirate's map), or figure out how far it is between your house and your best friend's.

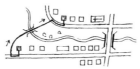

You could make your own maps to show where *you* had hidden something, or to mark the best route to the playground, or to show what the countryside is like around a vacation spot you've been to. Try it!

In the pages that follow, maps are used to show some important things about the continent you live on–North America–and the countries around you.

First is a map of the entire world, showing North America as only one among several other continents and with ocean around much of its border. This is a *political* map of the world, as the main thing it shows is the boundaries of all the separate countries. The projection used here to put the whole globe on flat paper is a different type than the one on page 7. Here *all* the spaces left when the globe was cut into sections are filled in.

The continent of North America is shown in three maps, each containing different information. The first is a *political* map, showing the countries in separate colors, each with their national flags.

The second is a *physical* and *land use* map, showing the nature of the land and the wild animals that live on it, and also the products man grows on it, such as The third is an *economic* map, showing the land's natural resources (such as oil and coal) and the products manufactured by large factories:

Each map has a legend to explain the many symbols used on it, and all three are in the same scale of 1:15,000,000.

A collection of maps is called an Atlas. Here is your very own Atlas of North America.

NORTH AMERICA

ATLANTIC OCEAN

PACIFIC OCEAN

SOUTH AMERICA

0   750

Scale 1: 75,000,000

Lake

River

Mountains

Wood

Tropical forest

Cultivated land

Grassland

Desert

Tundra

Ice

N

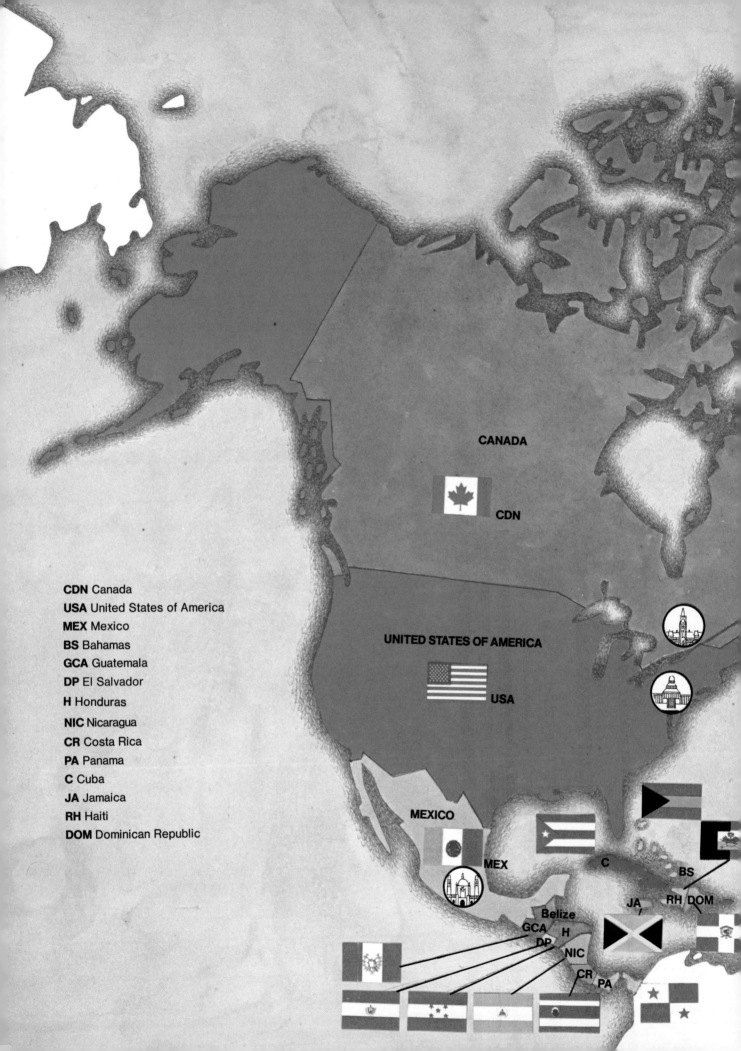

CDN Canada
USA United States of America
MEX Mexico
BS Bahamas
GCA Guatemala
DP El Salvador
H Honduras
NIC Nicaragua
CR Costa Rica
PA Panama
C Cuba
JA Jamaica
RH Haiti
DOM Dominican Republic

CANADA

CDN

UNITED STATES OF AMERICA

USA

MEXICO

MEX

C

BS

RH DOM

JA

Belize

GCA

DP

H

NIC

CR PA

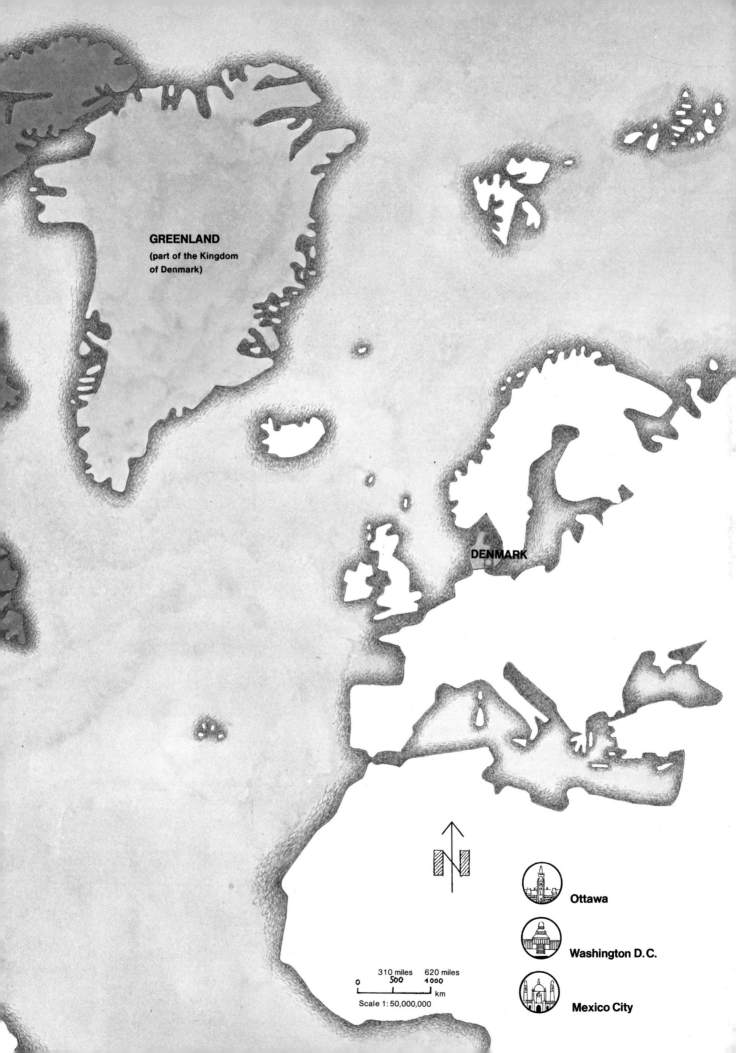

GREENLAND

(part of the Kingdom
of Denmark)

DENMARK

N

310 miles   620 miles

0   500   1000
                        km

Scale 1: 50,000,000

Ottawa

Washington D.C.

Mexico City

NORTH AND CENTRAL AMERICA

Ottawa
CANADA

Washington D.C.
UNITED STATES OF AMERICA

Mexico City
MEXICO

Guatemala City
GUATEMALA

San Salvador
EL SALVADOR

Tegucigalpa
HONDURAS

Managua
NICARAGUA

San-José
COSTA RICA

Panama City
PANAMA

Nassau
BAHAMAS

Havana
CUBA

Kingston
JAMAICA

Port-au-Prince
HAITI

Santo Domingo
DOMINICAN REPUBLIC

Borders

River

Lake

Forest

Deer   Wolves

Grizzly and polar bears

Musk-deer

Alligators

Forestry

Wheat, barley

Potatoes

Corn   Cotton

Tropical fruit   Sugar cane

Tobacco

Coffee   Cocoa

Pigs

Cattle

Sheep

Sharks

Whales

Gray-seal

Common-seal

Lobsters

Cod

Tuna

Salmon

Herring, sardines, mackerel

Oysters

62 miles   310 miles   620 miles

0   100   500   1000

km

Scale 1:35,000,000

Borders

Capital city

Mining

◄Petroleum refinery ►

Metal ores

Metallurgical industry

Automobile industry

Shipbuilding

Power station

Atomic research station

Chemical works

Textiles

Dairy and meat products

Lumber industry

Port

62 miles 310 miles 620 miles
0 100   500   1000
                          km

Scale 1:35,000,000